THE SCARIEST PLACES ON EARTH

ALCATRAZ

BY NICK GORDON

BELLWETHER MEDIA · MINNEAPOLIS, MN

Are you ready to take it to the extreme?
Torque books thrust you into the action-packed world
of sports, vehicles, mystery, and adventure. These
books may include dirt, smoke, fire, and chilling tales.
WARNING : read at your own risk.

Library of Congress Cataloging-in-Publication Data

Gordon, Nick.
Alcatraz / by Nick Gordon.
    pages cm. -- (Torque : the scariest places on earth)
 Includes bibliographical references and index.
 Summary: "Engaging images accompany information about Alcatraz. The combination of high-interest
subject matter and light text is intended for students in grades 3 through 7"--Provided by publisher.
 ISBN 978-1-60014-945-0 (hardcover: alk. paper)
1. United States Penitentiary, Alcatraz Island, California--Juvenile literature. 2. Alcatraz Island (Calif.)--
History--Juvenile literature. 3. Haunted prisons--California--Alcatraz Island--Juvenile literature. I. Title.
 HV9474.A4G67 2014
 365'.979461--dc23
                                                          2013007820

This edition first published in 2014 by Bellwether Media, Inc.

Printed in the United States of America, North Mankato, MN.

TABLE OF CONTENTS

CHAPTER 1

SOMETHING EVIL

Your footsteps echo through the prison halls. One cell door stands open. You step inside. A chill crawls up your spine. You feel as though you are being watched.

Something is in there. Something evil. You back out of the cell. A loud clang echoes through the halls. You scream. Will you escape the walls of Alcatraz?

CHAPTER 2

THE ROCK

Alcatraz Island sits in the misty San Francisco Bay. It is a small, rocky land. In 1853, the U.S. military built a fort on the island. The fort soon became a prison. Military prisoners were locked in cold, dark cells. Some believe their ghosts still haunt the prison grounds.

WHAT'S IN A NAME?

Spanish explorers came across Alcatraz Island in 1775. They named it *La Isla de los Alcatraces*. This means "Island of Pelicans." Prisoners later called it "The Rock."

Alcatraz receiving official approval in 1934

In 1934, Alcatraz **Federal Penitentiary** opened. It was made to be the harshest prison in the United States. It held some of the most dangerous criminals in the world. **Gangsters**, murderers, and other **inmates** lived within its walls. Some tried to escape. No one succeeded.

KEEP AWAY

The Miwok and Ohlone people lived near Alcatraz before European explorers arrived. They avoided the island. They believed evil spirits lived there.

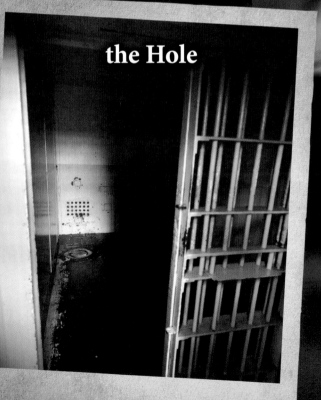

CHAPTER 3
ANGRY SPIRITS

Guards and prisoners told strange tales about Alcatraz. They spoke of unexplained voices, chills, and feelings. Many reported seeing the ghost of a man from the 1800s. Was it the spirit of a military prisoner still trapped within the prison walls?

the Hole

GET IN THE HOLE!

The worst place in Alcatraz was the Hole. Prisoners in this cell were completely shut out. They had only a dim light and meals of bread and water.

11

One famous story tells of an evil spirit called the Thing. One night, an inmate was sent to the Hole. He soon began to scream. He said he was being attacked by something with glowing eyes. The inmate begged the guards to let him out. They ignored him. Later, the cell grew quiet.

Guards entered the cell in the morning. The man was dead! His face was twisted into a horrible **grimace**. Doctors said that he had been **strangled**. The guards believed that the Thing had killed him. The next day, the guards did a **head count**. The dead man was in the lineup! The guards stared. Then, the man disappeared.

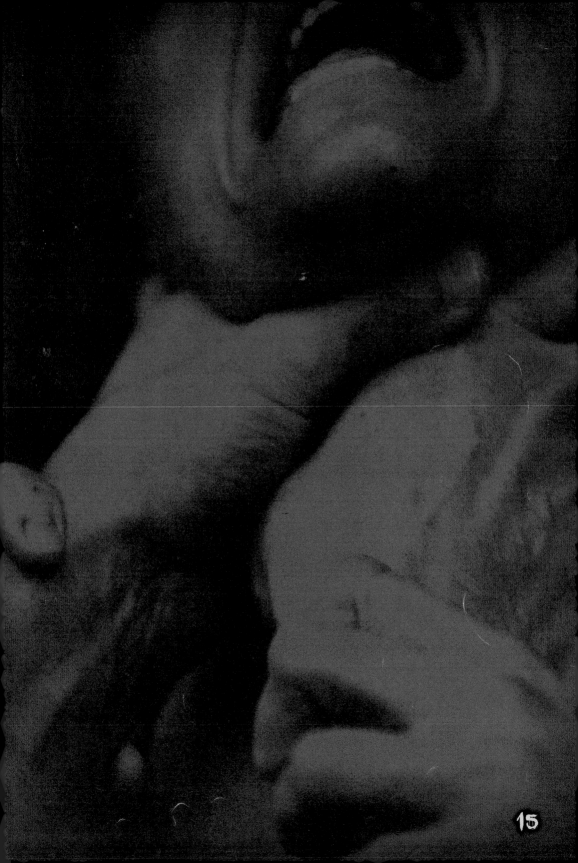

Al Capone

A PRISONER'S SONG

Alcatraz's most famous prisoner was gangster Al Capone. He was known to play the banjo during his time on The Rock. Visitors today claim to hear his ghostly music.

Many inmates could not handle the harsh life at Alcatraz. The days were long and silent. It drove prisoners **insane**. One chopped off all of the fingers on his left hand. Another tried to slash his own throat with a pair of eyeglasses. He was later killed as he tried to escape.

CHAPTER 4

GHOSTS OF ALCATRAZ

Alcatraz Federal Penitentiary closed in 1963. Today, tourists visit the old prison by day. Alcatraz is dark and silent at night. But many believe it isn't empty. Tour guides have heard running footsteps, voices, and even screams. When they search the halls, no one is there.

THE THREE INMATES

In 1946, several inmates tried to take over their cell house. Three of them were killed in the battle. Years after the prison closed, a night watchman heard clanging sounds. They were coming from the old hallway where the three inmates had died.

Many visitors have reported strange sights and sounds at Alcatraz. Some feel chills or sense something evil. Do the ghosts of the nation's worst criminals still linger there? The bodies of the prisoners are long gone. But could Alcatraz still imprison their souls?

GLOSSARY

cell—a small room in which a prisoner is held

federal penitentiary—a prison that holds criminals found guilty of serious crimes

fort—a military post

gangsters—members of a gang of violent criminals

grimace—a face that shows extreme pain

head count—a practice in which prison guards count each prisoner to make sure no one is missing

inmates—people locked in a prison

insane—unable to properly understand reality

strangled—killed by choking

tourists—people who travel to visit another place

TO LEARN MORE

AT THE LIBRARY

Gordon, Nick. *Eastern State Penitentiary*. Minneapolis, Minn.: Bellwether Media, 2014.

Hawkins, John. *Hauntings*. New York, N.Y.: PowerKids Press, 2012.

Person, Stephen. *Ghostly Alcatraz Island*. New York, N.Y.: Bearport Pub. Co., 2011.

ON THE WEB

Learning more about Alcatraz is as easy as 1, 2, 3.

1. Go to www.factsurfer.com.

2. Enter "Alcatraz" into the search box.

3. Click the "Surf" button and you will see a list of related Web sites.

With factsurfer.com, finding more information is just a click away.

INDEX

The images in this book are reproduced through the courtesy of: Kenkistler, front cover (bottom), pp. 20-21; Sergioboccardo, front cover (top), pp. 2-3 (background), 6-7; Croisy, front cover & p. 21 (skull); David Clapp/ Getty Images, pp. 4-5; Kropic1, p. 7 (top); Everett Collection Inc/ Alamy, p. 8; Ingo Schulz/ imagebrok/ Imagebroker.net/ SuperStock, p. 10; Dan Lee, p. 11; Maridav, pp. 12-13; Joe Belanger, p. 14; PhotoAlto/ SuperStock, p. 15; Album/ Album/ SuperStock, p. 16; gosphotodesign, p. 17 (left); Mark Scott, p. 17 (right); E.J. Baumeister Jr./ Alamy, p. 18; Associated Press, p. 19.